LETTERS OF THE HIGH MEDIEVAL RUSSIAN CHURCH

Translated by: Tatiana Ivanovich, D.P. Curtin

Copyright @ 2023 Dalcassian Press

All rights reserved. No part of this publication may be reproduced, distributed, or transmitted in any form or by any means, including photocopying, recording, or other electronic or mechanical methods, without the prior written permission of the publisher, except in the case of brief quotations embodied in critical reviews and certain other non-commercial uses permitted by copyright law. For permission request, write to Dalcassian Press at dalcassianpublishing at gmail.com

ISBN: 979-8-8691-3761-6 (Paperback)

Library of Congress Control Number:
Author: Curtin, D.P. (1985-)

Printed by Ingram Content Group, 1 Ingram Blvd, La Vergne, Tennessee

First printing edition 2023.

LETTERS OF THE HIGH MEDIEVAL RUSSIAN CHURCH

LETTER FROM METROPOLITAN THEOGNOST TO CHERVLENY YAR, TO THE BASKAKS, CLERGY AND LAITY
About the limits of the dioceses, Ryazan and Sarai

Blessing of Theognostos, Metropolitan of All Rus', to my children, to the Baskak and to the centurion, and to the abbot and to the priest, and to all the Christians of Cherleny Yar and to all the city, along the Great Crow. I pray to God and the Holy Mother of God, may you be good in soul and body, may you be healthy, and may you fulfill the natural commandments of God, may you have natural love for your neighbor and for everyone, alms according to your strength, truth, chastity, confession of your sins, and heirs without end eternal kingdom. You will be God's. And you know, children, in ancient days there were speeches and rebellion between the two Lords, Ryazan and Sarai, about this question of redistribution, and he sent his abbot to you, so that he would consider in truth, what redistribution will look like. According to the same abbot's obedience, I gave a letter to the Lord of Saransk, Afonasius. Now the Vladyka of Ryazan came to me with his kriloshans and brought to me a letter from my brother Maxim the Metropolitan, and another letter from my brother Peter the Metropolitan, and they ruled the Vladyka of Ryazan and ordered him to hold the entire frontier along the Great Crow. He showed us the third letter of the Lord of Sarai Sophony, somehow, he retreated from that front that he could not enter, not the Sarai frontier, but the Ryazan frontier. And seeing how they spoke, I judged, according to those letters of my brother Metropolitans, that the Lord of Ryazan should hold the redistribution of all that, along with the Great Crow. And even if he had seen these letters before, he would not have sent the abbot to inquire, nor would he have given the letter to the Lord of Sarai. And now I have put that letter aside; but I cannot destroy the letter of my brother Metropolitans. And that's why, now I'm writing to you,, according to those letters of my brotherhood, the Metropolitans govern the Vladyka of Ryazan, and the whole redistribution, according to the Great Crow, is moving forward; and the Lord of Sarai has no need to intercede. I gave the rightful charter to the Lord of Ryazan Kiril, just as my brothers gave the Metropolitans. And you have love for him, and all obedience and submission, and do everything that is said to you, helpful and saved. What will be the church tax, otherwise give it to him, according to long-standing church custom? May the mercy of God and the Holy Mother of God, and my blessing be with you.

LETTER OF GRANT FROM THE RYAZAN GRAND DUKE OLEG IOANNOVICH TO THE OLGOV MONASTERY

For the village of Arestovskoye, confirming the right to own graveyards, fields and other lands given to the monastery from his ancestors and boyars

By the mercy of God and the prayer of the Holy Mother of God, and the prayer of my father the Great Prince Ivan Oleksandrovich, and the blessing of the Bishop of Ryazan and Murom Vasily, I am the Great Prince Oleg Ivanovich, having guessed with my father with the Lord with Vasily and with his boyars (and the boyars were with me: Sophony Altykulachevich, Semyon Fedorovich, Mikita Andreevich, Timosh Oleksandrovich, Manasya uncle, Yury Okolnichy, Yury Chashnik, Semyon Mikitich with his brother, Pavel Sorobich), I gave to my father Arseny the monastery of the Holy Mother of God, in Olgov its independence, he is free to bless anyone to become abbot. I gave the Holy Mother of God to the house of Arestovskoe village, with wines, and with red-handed, and with cuttings, and with sixty, and with all duties, and with beekeepers with bee lands, with manure, lakes, beavers, and with its overhangs. And having grown up in this letter, with my father, with the Lord, with Vasily and with the boyars: since our ancestors raised the Holy Mother of God, Prince the Great Ingvar, Prince Oleg, Prince Yuri, and with them the boyars 300 (ͳ), and the husband 600 (Х); then they gave the Holy Mother of God to the house 9 (ⷪ) land lands, and 5 (є) churchyards, Pesochna, and in it 500 (ҭ) families, Kholokholna, and in it one and a half hundred families, Zayachina, and in it 200 (ҫ) families, Vepriya 200 (ҫ) families, Zayachkov 100 and 60 (р and ӟ) families; and all the churchyards are with lands, with cut-offs, and with manure, and with lakes, beavers, overhangs, cuttings with sixty, and with wines, with red-handed, and with all duties. And who are the people who were given by our ancestors to the Holy Mother of God in the house where they have peasants, or beekeepers, or settlements, in my fatherland, and they know the house of the Holy Mother of God. My lords do not intercede with them about anything. Fyodor Borisovich gave Golovchin, and Clement gave Danilov's yard to Mordovskaya, and Erem the Great and Gleb gave their villages to the Lady of the Theotokos, and the men of the Olgovskaya on the outskirts, who bought from the Murom Princes, gave 300 (ҭ) hryvnia, and gave to the Holy Mother of God. The Grand Duke Oleg Ivanovich gave the Arestovskoye village to the Holy Mother of God to the house, and all that our ancestors held, with places and people. What did the boyars give to the house of the Holy Mother of God? I want to pursue this, and not to offend anyone at the house of the Holy Mother of God. Yet, the volostels, and the tributaries, and the coachmen do not borrow from the people of the Mother of God for anything else. Whoever harms the house of the Holy Mother of God, or the Prince, or the Lord, or the volost, or whoever is different must answer before God the Holy Lady Theotokos. When I left my fatherland, on my own, from Pereyaslavl, I made a vow, to the Holy Lady Theotokos I gave the Ryazan village and the coastal one, even to give [...] in my fatherland [...] in Pereyaslavl.

LETTER FROM METROPOLITAN ALEXY TO CHERVLENY YAR, TO THE BOYARS, BASKAKS, CLERGY AND LAITY
On their jurisdiction to the Ryazan Bishop

Blessing of Alexey, Metropolitan of All Russia, to all the peasants who are found in the front of Cherleny Yar and on guard near Khopory, to the Don, to the priest and deacon, and to the Baskak, and to the centurion, and to the boyars. I pray to God and the Holy Mother of God, may you all be good in soul and body, may you be healthy, may you fulfill the natural commandments of

God; for Christ said: "I have my commandments and keep them, and love me." May you be loved by Christ and fulfill his commandments. Have faith in the right to the holy and consubstantial Trinity, being baptized in the first place, love and peace for each other, truth, chastity, alms, confession of your sins; for the Lord God Jesus Christ thus declared as his disciple and Apostle: "Going into all the world, preach the Gospel to every creature; Whoever has faith and is baptized will be saved, but he who does not believe will be condemned." And again he gave them the same grace and power: "If you bind on earth (sin for the sake of man), you will be bound in heaven; "As much as you permit it on earth, there will be permission in heaven." And again, he says: "By listening to you, he listens to me, and by rejecting you, he is rejecting me." The same grace of the Most Holy Spirit was received by the sinners from the Most Reverend Patriarch of the Ecumenical and from the Holy Assembly, and I came to St. Sophia, in the Metropolitan of All Rus', to Kiev, and to all the Christians found throughout the Russian land as a teacher. I have a great burden on myself that I should speak and teach everyone about everything that is beneficial for salvation. And for this reason, the Metropolitan wrote to you many times, to his children, as far as it is for the benefit of your souls. You have shown that you do not listen to my words and my teaching but fulfill your bodily will and dark matters. You do not listen to my words. Don't you know that all the Russian lands of the Lord are under my power and in my will? And I present them by the grace of the Holy Spirit. Power has also been given to your Master. You still don't accept his word; but you receive strange shepherds. Somehow it seems that there is no one from the flock of the true shepherd, Christ, but an opposing spirit: for the verbal sheep of Christ listen to the voice of Christ and follow our words. We are Christ's and we speak Christ's words: Who is Christ, who listens to us and creates as much as I write. Whoever does not listen to us is not God: for a true Christian and faithful in his works is, like the Apostle, saying: "Faith without works is dead, and so are works without faith." For this reason, children, do the deeds of light; For let all malice and bitterness and wrath and wrath, fornication and adultery, resentment and envy, murder and drunkenness be taken away from you, for the Apostle said: "Brothers, do not be enticed, neither by harlots, nor by adulterers, nor by idolaters, nor by those who commit sexual immorality with your own hands, neither the adulterers, nor the covetous, nor the Tateves, nor the robbers of the kingdom of God will inherit." Hearing these things, lovers, always from the Saints, repent and turn to God, learn to create good things and watch for yourself; remember death and resurrection, and this terrible judgment and this great and terrible Judge, who knows the human heart and thoughts and deeds, and eternal peace for the righteous, and eternal torment for the sinner. If you remember all that, you will never sin or disobey us, who have set the Holy Spirit as shepherds and teachers to all the peasants. Always run to the churches, with your wives and children, and bring whatever you have in your hands to the churches and to the saints; but love the priests and ministers and ask for their prayers; Have mercy on the widow, and the orphan, and the populace, and the strange; visit those in prison, so that you may be worthy of that blessed holy voice of the true Christ, saying: "The blessings of my Father will come, and inherit the kingdom prepared for you from the foundation of the world. I was hungry, and you fed me. I was thirsty, give me drink. I was a stranger and you welcomed me. I was sick and in prison, and you visited me;" and the evil and lawless, and the unmerciful, and the merciless, pour them into the outer darkness. Whatever you have to do, you will be saved, and it will not be hard. About the same question of redistribution, along the Great Vorona, near Khopor, to the Don on guard, the church that he redistributed, how to write letters from my brother Maxim the Metropolitan, Peter, and Theognostus, that the Assembly was held in Kostroma. Vladyka Sophony gave letters from his own mouth, and from those places. According to those letters, he should not intercede in that foreign frontier, and it has been revealed and everyone knows that that frontier is not Saraisky. Now Vladyka Athanasius of Sarai knew that, having seen their letter, and for his guilt, he was punished by the Metropolitan with a letter, and he renounced that redistribution. From now on, Lord Aeonasius of Sarai has no power in that realm, but only the power of Rezan, the priests and deacons who supply the Lord and give that power. And now I have sent Vladyka Vasily of Ryazan to you with his letter. You must remember him and give him the church tithe according to custom. Fulfill what I am writing to you, for your spiritual benefit, and you will listen to the certificates, and you will also give the church its funds. The mercy of God, the Holy Mother of God, and my blessing be with you, and with your wives, children, and with all Christians.

Message of the Patriarch of Constantinople Nile to the Pskovites
About the Strigolniki.

Noble and honest boyars, men of Pskov, my son the mayor, and all others, my children and other people of Christ's name, subject to the holy metropolis of all Rus', in the Russian city of Pskov and within its borders. Children of the Lord, beloved of our humility, I call you all sons and children, and also you, who have separated from the Catholic Church and the Christian community, have apostatized, by the action of an evil demon. Having already seen our humility and our greatness, the Holy Hierarch, the Divine Assembly, who is not from you, knows of piety, who intends to preserve the divine Scripture and the sacred canon, those heretics, having excommunicated the apostolic council churches, saints and priests and all clergy and others Christian people, who supply everything, consider only the faithful for themselves. Having heard this, we were deeply saddened in our hearts and inwardly about the cutting off of Christ's hearts, which we do not wish to suffer, hearing our hearts being cut off from the enemy of truth, who was the original enemy of mankind, championing our base nature. This is his disposition always: whenever it is not possible for him to actually fraternize, he implicitly informs our imagination. Thus, you introduced all of this heresy into the Church of Christ. Since the coming of Christ, all idolatry has passed away without a trace, and the devil has had no place other than to subjugate people to idolatry, moving from the right hand of our brothers. It is clearly not possible to deceive but many worship God, calling the Son of God a creation. Such other heresies were introduced from the right hand, who in the process acquired polytheism. And today we see that it is happening in you, but little by little you will be set aside from Christianity and the priesthood, which the saints and clergy have given to the people, without which it is impossible to have any hope of salvation. Even more so, an angel lives on earth and this false praise dwells in us. He will create faith, just as he creates the order according to the reward of the Church of God. And who is the evil demon who deceives them so much that they can accept such a thing? For the Catholic Apostolic Church of God, which abides from end-to-end, is immovably strengthened by the grace and power of Christ our God Himself in orthodoxy. Such are the sacred canons, the presence and structure of those who practice simony are known, as if selling the unsold grace of the All-Holy Spirit, with Simon and with Macedonia and with others he considers them to be Doukhoborts. Because of these things, the Church of Christ always thinks in this way. Because this wickedness is active and daring to establish itself, there is no structure, and there is no cathedral church. The essence of the matter is that it works secretly, without knowing anything, but when they are convicted, they suffer, as if from the church, they are condemned and reproached. And even if there are no bishops, they are creators by virtue of their appointment: but it is not appropriate for this to cut them off from the church and welcome all heretics, but united as a communicant of the church, and to report the evil of the Bishop to his Metropolitan. If he does not make corrections, he will be excluded from our humility, which God established as our father and teacher, the Ecumenical Patriarch of Constantinople. For this reason, we write and inform you in a fatherly manner, as if you were our children. For by the participation of the church, as Christ himself, who is the head of the whole church, ceases from strife and separation, and unites, with one mind, and gives glory to the rest of the church. For the Church of Christ is glorified in its orthodoxy and in its true life; and even if the church has money, it clearly denounces dishonesty. The historians themselves supply many such occurrences for candles, for wine and other duties, and for rags. The church is not hurt by this, for this has happened hence, just as said by Christ: "Freely you have received, now freely give." It is necessary to collect money for setting up a business; otherwise, it is about the necessary needs of history. And we find the Lord our God Jesus Christ, who goes to many houses with his disciples and is worthy of receiving him, who teaches the true word and the understanding of God, and performs many miracles, receiving what happens from them; and sowing in abundance. "When the publican went into the house of Matthew, he said, and made him a great man." And: "I entered into the house of Mary and Martha, and Martha was anxious to perform many services," and many others were found. The holy Apostle Paul, citing from the Law of Moses, said: "Thou shalt not bind the mouth of the ox," interpreting the same reason of the Divine Scripture, "always about the will, speech, God forbids, but for us to speak everything." Also: "the sacred food from the church is eaten. The altar servants are separated from the altar." Thus, the Lord commanded those who preach the Gospel to live. "If we bring you all spiritual gifts, is it better if we reap your bodily benefits?" Although there is much that can be found in the Divine Scripture, even if it is achieved with right reason and a good conscience, it does nothing to create an order that is created without compensation. Even though you understand everything, try to correct the evil that has happened. For this reason, for the sake of the ambassador, our humility and the great Assembly of the God-loving Archbishop of Suzdal, Dionysius, an honest and pious and virtuous husband, and a well-known guardian of the sacred canons. May you see from us both to bless, and to teach and to punish, and to inform and arrange similar things, to unite with those born in the apostolic church of God. Let us know that by excommunication from the church, that very presence of Christ our God is excommunicated. They can have no part in either the lot, neither in this world nor in the future. Which church will you come to? Neither the Latin Church, nor any other than the apostolic and paternal faiths according to the commission, there and this happens. Truly, the Pope brings money to the church. If you separate yourself from your church, you are cut off like heretics because of the reward of the establishment; then Christ will no longer have a church on earth today, according to your word, and a lie is spoken, for he says: "as I am with you until the end of the age." But there is no other way. Do not follow this path. May you, having known the path of salvation and united with your brothers, glorify God in one union, whose grace and mercy may be with all of you. This was written by many here, but more was written by Archbishop Dionysius: "Before we can speak from our lips, accept our word." And you wish, write to us, and let us rejoice in the correction that was by the grace of God. Let us glorify God and rejoice in the return of those and in their repentance, in which angels and men rejoice, according to the words of our Lord Jesus Christ, who may we all receive mercy and love for humanity, in this also in the future, to him be glory with the Father and with the Holy Spirit, now and ever and unto ages of ages, Amen.

STATUTORY CHARTER OF SUZDAL ARCHBISHOP DIONYSIUS TO THE SNETOGORSK MONASTERY
On compliance with the rules of the monastic community

I hasten to God and confirm the word, for the sake of the Word, and fulfill the Holy Spirit, as the commandments of the all-holy Ecumenical Patriarch, caring for the souls of men, to teach and punish and rule, according to the divine commandments of the Gospel, to strengthen and bless the living, who has turned aside, to return to the right path. For a virtuous life, having tired out the holy and God-bearing Fathers, the common life, according to the great

Pachomius, the angel of God, and according to the Great Basil, the two ranks of the inscribed life, the deserted and the common life, the hedgehog was praised more than the deserted one, and Saint Ephraim. Thus he writes, with Saint John the divine ladder, especially affirmed and decorated with various wisdom of punishments. I have come, by the message of the all-holy Patriarch of the Ecumenical, to the God-protected city of Pskov, about the correction of those who have separated from the collective apostolic church of Christ and for the establishment and correction of the priest and the honest monastery and all people named for Christ, and hearing about the honorable monastery of the Most Holy Theotokos, also called Snetnaya Gora, living in common, and our souls rejoiced greatly and rejoiced greatly. With diligence I breathed, and saw, and was blessed by the Ecumenical Patriarch, and I found, uncorrected in all things, the Divine Scripture and the God-bearing statutes of the Father, creating and leaving behind. About the divine common life, the fulfillment of the monastic rule, and about the height of dispassion. I begged the venerable abbot, who exists and is brothers in Christ, to guide those who have gone astray and to punish those who are not punished. I am Dionysius Archbishop of Suzdal, by order of the all-holy Patriarch of the Ecumenical, having risen in the Nomocanon, in the rules of the holy Fathers, even about the divine common life. I have seen priestly rules neglected, to offend the holy Father restrictions. As the holy rule was stated in the 5th Assembly: "It is fitting for me to have nothing of my own, but to hand everything of my own over to the monastery's authority." The speech of the Godly Luke about those who believed in Christ and corrected the life of Manish: "for not one person has anything from his own word of his being, but it is common to all." Moreover, those who want to meet, come together and specify your needs. After tonsure, those who join him in the monastery will have power. They are not allowed to worry about anything about themselves or to behave in this way. If anyone buys some acquisitions that are not part of the monastery, creating his own, let it be accepted by the abbot or bishop, and with much boldness we will sell it to both the poor and let such acquisitions be heard among the weak and ill. Ananya, having learned to steal, commanded the holy Assembly to be wise about the prohibition brought about. If we take silver for our own, having not laid it all at the feet of the apostles, we die. What is proper to say about those who do not offer everything to themselves to God, but part of them work with their own lusts, and they will find greater languor, as if the spirit of God is strong and body and destroy? This is true even in the holy image of those who live in the monasteries, and speak not a word. This is yours, and this is mine, or this and that; for the five thousand monks are simple, and everything is common to the name, no one has his own thing. Moreover, in the general life of the monastery, they cannot be named, and say "this is mine". Where the creeping nuance of the weeds sown by the devil has grown up in common life, it is not worthy of being called common, but the thief of the seat, and the theft of sacred things and all evils are hostile to the workers. For this reason, it will be called a common life, to hold everything in common, and not a single one to have the devil's undertakings in his own care, less they become dirty and insane, as Great Basil said: "as if you have something of your own in the monasteries in your cell, great or small, something alien to God's churches, the Lord's love is will be a stranger. It is more beneficial to live with those of little intelligence, rather than with many homeless people, who transgress the commandments of the Lord." Now they have fallen into this great sin, and the rules of the saints have been violated, the Father is guilty of ignorance. If they begin to repent worthily and promise not to fall into the same great sin, as the humble Archbishop Dionysius of Suzdal, with the blessing of the all-holy Patriarch, they may be forgiven.

Henceforth, by order of the all-holy Patriarch of the Ecumenical, in honor seven monasteries of the Holy Mother of God, on Snetnaya Hora, by statute, this monastery, for its honor will maintain nothing of its own, neither to the abbot nor to the brethren, but to give everything to God and the Holy Mother of God. You must neither eat nor drink in the cell, and do not ask the cellarer. Do not give anything to the cellarer, or give anything to anyone without the abbot's word. Eat and drink at the meal together with everyone. Again, neither eat nor drink at all, neither before dinner or after lunch; but don't drink when you're drunk. Get the clothes you need from the abbot, ordinary ones, not German clothes. Wear woolen fur coats without down, and wear shoes and shoes from the abbot. Do not keep extra clothes. And in the church, according to the rule and the regulation of the saints, let the Father sing. And wherever he is sent to serve, go with him without disobedience. You cannot go anywhere without the abbot's blessing. Obedience and submission have in all respects to the abbot. If anyone begins to speak against the abbot and start quarrels, he will be locked in prison until he repents. The disobedient man, according to the first, second and third punishment, will be sent out of the monastery, and they will not give him anything from what he brought into the monastery. Behold, it is not enough for me to write to you; and the rest you will find in the books of St. Basil the Great of Caesarea, and St. Ephraim, and St. Ivan Climacus, and St. Theodore of Studiya and other saints, about obedience and humility and other virtues that have already been accomplished. The Holy Mother of God and the blessing of God will receive the All-Holy Patriarch of the Ecumenical church, and she is bestowing blessings, and God has prepared much for those who love him. Our ears listen and behold, as the patron of this honorable monastery, the rector, having created this monastery and united the brothers, and by its charter introduced the saints. He, creating a common life, announced with many punishments and confirmed with many oaths, the salvation of human souls, abiding to this monastery, honorably, and to all people named for Christ, and for the benefit and praise of those who reside in this God-protected city of Pskov. Here, renewing, I write for the approval of this charter, as if anyone would dare to think of turning this good instruction into an evil custom, will be under the burden of excommunication of the Most Holy Patriarch Vselensky.

MESSAGE OF PATRIARCH ANTHONY OF CONSTANTINOPLE TO THE PSKOVITES
About the denunciation of Strigolniks

Patriarch Anthony, by the grace of God, Archbishop of Constantinagrad [Constantinople], new Rome, and Ecumenical Patriarch. O God-loving Bishop of Velikago of Novagrad, and your supporting archbishopric of Piskovgrad and other borders, to your noble mayor, lord and all the boyars, to the nuns and monks, and all the people of the Lord's name in Christ! Our humility and the divine and sacred Assembly, which is providential for you, according to its duty. Everywhere the Christians do not cease to write and teach about the faith, leading to peace and their salvation. For this purpose, to introduce with zeal and diligence to the Russians, and to punish many people and pacify the many great temptations that have preceded from the envy of the evil demon, we have already announced you, to our humility and to the entire sacred Assembly that presides, about the heresies that were previously brewing there with you. These are schismatic, because you were tempted at the time of this by a certain Carp, a deacon excommunicated from service, a strigolnik, who said: "you are not worthy of the priesthood that we supply. It is unworthy to receive communion from them, nor to repent to them, nor to receive baptism from them." We were confused and offended by this, leading to spiritual trouble, and born in the same depression, and with the bewilderment of the crooked demon. Therefore, we were surprised, and other temptations were brought to us. For this reason, we sent our humility and the great Assembly of the God-loving Archbishop of Suzdal, Dionysius, to you with letters. He is a man of honest and pious and virtuous, and a guardian of the sacred liturgy. May you see this from us and bless you, and teach and show, and gather together all the members and apostles of the church. Let everyone know that by being excommunicated from the church, that Christ himself is being excommunicated. They have no part, no sacred lot from him, neither in this world nor in the future, as the Lord said in the holy Gospels to his disciple and Apostle, and according to them to the Christian teacher: "those listening to you, listen to me; and by sweeping you away, they sweep me away." The Fathers expounded the holy and God-bearing words, inspired by the Holy Spirit, and after falling and rising through corruption, to follow the unpretentious and right path. Therefore, you too, O Strigolnitsy, correct yourselves, especially of these heresies, having seen the evil that has fallen on you. Submit to your elders and repent of your sins, and retreat from your heresies. I say, behold, your father, the Patriarch. Unite in goodness, in humility, and love for the people, the servants of God. Give the church of God due obedience. And as long as there is no sin, having escaped God's love for mankind, and even if you confess that you have naturally sinned, ask for forgiveness and mercy from the ministers of the saints of the church. And God, who laid down the law for the Apostles, like the Apostle Paul, said: "Repent to your elders, so that you may watch over your souls, for they will repay the word against you on the day of judgment" (for goodness' sake), let them forgive you all your sins. Otherwise, you will not be broken-hearted and humble, but you will remain insubordinate even to the end, in your disobedience and cruelty. No one will separate you from us, even if excommunication has been declared against you. And if anyone, by speaking against the priests, causes a schism among the Christians, let him be damned. And God said: "I have prepared for you a dwelling place, and not paradise; Heaven is a holy place, like a church altar." The Church is an entrance for everyone, because we are mothers who give birth to everything through holy baptism and nourish everything that lives without difficulty in it, clothing and cheering everyone who dwells in it. As the Prophet said: "All the working churches will eat and be satisfied." And again: "O children of the church, having sucked the fat and ointment of her, anoint your heads with gladness." And as David said: "Your house will be drunk with abundance, and I will feed your food with a stream." And again, about the priest's clothing and the vestment: "Your priests will be clothed with righteousness." And again, the Lord said: "like Cain, who was not sanctified, he was jealous of the sacred Abel for the sacred rank and killed him with envy." And then the Lord said: "Woe to those who sin! For this reason, I destroyed the beastial spirit with the soul." But like from the tree of wisdom, if you take it down [...] understand neither good nor evil. With such malice and deceitful words the devil deceived the human race, and we departed from the living tree. God, who created us, with indescribable bounties, gave us communion of the holy, most pure mysteries, the true fruit of the animal, which we eat and live forever. And now the devil does not cease deceiving the human race: then the glory of God itself fell away and was separated from the tree of life. Now Strigolnika has been excommunicated from service and expelled from the church in favor of the orthodox faith; and slandered the entire Ecumenical Assembly, Patriarchs and Metropolitans and Bishops, and abbots and priests and the entire sacred order. They said that they were not appointed according to their worthy post. Through such guilt, the evil-minded deceivers are excommunicated from the communion of the holy, most pure, life-giving mysteries of Christ, and put a charm greater than the charms of a serpent. For serpents are deceitful, and otherwise they die by death. Through this delusion one goes into eternal torment. The Lord himself said: "Heaven and earth pass by, but my words will not pass by." I "Whoever eats my flesh and drinks my blood, remains in me." "Unless you have eaten the flesh of the Son of man, nor have you drunk his blood, you shall not have life within you." The Strigolnitsy, opponents of Christ, command, as if from the tree of life, to withdraw from communion [...] showing them the scriptures of the book, which were copied, to help their heresy, in order to set the people against the priests, likening them to Korah, Dathan, and Abiron, who set against Moses and Aron, saying: "bring sanctifications to God, for we are also priests". He sent 250 people away to follow him; and Moses said to them: "Try for yourselves new censers and put fire in them, I will bring them before God: as the Lord wills, so it will be." They disobeyed, took upon themselves the priesthood and dignity, bringing forth the temian and sang before the temple of the witness. The Lord God was angry with them, and commanded the earth to kill and devour them, with their wives and with their children, and they went down to hell. Those who remained were burned with fire. Then Moses and Aaron established the old law: the foundation and image became the new law of Christ. Then Korah, and Dathan and Abiron, themselves supposedly priests, raised the people against the saints, and led them towards the living hell. In the same way, even now, strigolnitsa, who neither possess priesthood nor hierarchical rank, are themselves appointed as teachers by the people, out of vanity and arrogance, and those who listen to them lead to destruction. Christ our God saved twelve disciples and these apostles, having prayed to God and the Father, laid his hands on them, and commanded them to teach the nations. The apostles, seeing the faith of Christ spreading, the teaching of the Word growing, elected his disciples and appointed them as a bishop, created by the Patriarch (and laid down the following rules: "Establish two or three bishops"). The bishops said to the Patriarch: before death he was, he ordered this matter, so that the priesthood would not die with them. The Apostles themselves took ordination from Christ the Son of God, and also gave ordination by the Patriarch and Metropolitan and other priests. According to that rule, to this day, Patriarchs and Metropolitans elect each region and appoint a Patriarch, and the Patriarch and Metropolitans appoint a Metropolitan; The Metropolitan with the Bishops appoints the bishop, and the Bishop with the priests and deacons appoints the priests and deacons: and so it is worthy for us to have every priest as an Apostle of Christ. When a priest performs the service, they are as Christ in Zion, having supper with the disciples. Thus, it is worthy to receive communion from his hand, as it is from the hand of Christ having supper. And do not reason or inquire about the Jews, whether you are worthy or not. The great teacher of the earth, Paul wrote these words to the Corinthians: "Let man first judge himself, let him eat from the bread and drink from the cup, and let him not eat and sing without judgment, without judging the body and blood of Christ." Look at this, the strigolnitsy are especially heretical, for just as the Apostle Paul said, "consider for yourself, and not as the Jews". Or do you say: "are the unworthy spirit sellers?" Christ, who knew Judas, who wanted to betray him at the supper, did not condemn him before the judgment. Who are you who judge someone else's slave? His Lord either stands or falls. God is able to raise him up. Where do you want to get your priest? If you say: "the Patriarch is unworthy and the Metropolitan is unworthy"; then, according to your words, now, there is not a single priest on earth, even if he, having shared poverty, is without church gifts. But we confess with our thoughts and faith, and we all partake of the synods and apostles of the church. We shall consecrate him the Metropolitan, the Patriarch, whom we all honor as the vicar of Christ, as well as the bishop in every city and region, the priests as the Apostles of Christ. According to your divine faith, where do you have a priest? Christ would not come again to descend upon the earth, nor would an Angel descend to sanctify your priest; Even if an angel sanctified a priest for you, then it is not appropriate for him to believe, according to the Apostle Paul, who said: "If an angel preaches to you more good news than what is preached, he will be cursed." How can we humiliate the saint with the church protors, who collect from those supplied. A church reproach should be, according to the Apostle Paul, who says: "The churchman feeds on the church and the altar boys share with the altar? Whoever plants grapes, let him not eat its fruit; Should anyone feed a flock, but let him not eat some of its milk? The worker is worthy to receive his reward." Christ, our God, saved when he called Matthew from the tollhouse, who became the Apostles in his rank. He created great fear in his house, not only honoring the one Christ, and the Apostles, but by many people, sinners and tax collectors. Then Christ himself said: "I did not come to call the righteous, but sinners to repentance." Even if you, scoundrels and heretics, consider yourself righteous, don't you hear the Apostle saying: "If we say, there is no sin, we lie and there is no truth in us"? Because of the commandment, you, Strigolians, rise up against the saints and priests, wanting to seize the honor for yourself. Study the words of the book, which are sweet to hear as Christians, and become teachers of the people. And do not remember the words of Christ, who said: "Do not enter by the door into the sheepfold, but by entering through the door, they might be a thief." Everyone who does not have a holy position, tries to teach, and reproaches the teacher, did not enter through the door. Thieves and robbers kill people with weapons, but you, Strigolnitsy, kill people with the death of wisdom, the removal for the sake of the most pure mysteries of the body and blood of Christ. Christ, our God spoke: "If anyone does not eat my flesh, neither drink my blood, nor have light nor life; death will be on the last day." Have you become like him with the mark: "And having heard this word, you went back from Hrieth and went with no one." Do you not understand, Strigolnitsy, that it is written in the Holy Gospel: "When Christ supped with his disciples, he broke the bread and gave it to the disciples, saying: Take and eat, this is my body, which was broken for you for many times, for the remission of sins; then I accepted the cup of wine and gave praise, saying to my disciples: drink of it, all of you, behold, this is my blood of the New Testament: behold, do this in my recollection?" In the same way, even to this day, priests perform services in remembrance of the salvific passion of Christ. If anyone moves away from these most pure mysteries, then he is not a true Christian unless he listens to the Lord God who says: "Whoever eats my flesh and drinks my blood, the wound remains in me." The Strigolnitsy say about the present-day saints and about the priests: 'they are unworthy of those services, as [...]' they take from Christians the offering given to them, both for the living and for the dead. But God does not understand that it is worthy to accept from those who give alms. For Christ himself came to the house of Zacchaeus to dine and received what was given. If Christ had not received a name from anyone, why would the disciples go to buy bread in the city of Samaria, while Christ sat in the storehouse? And what kind of silver would Judas carry in the ark? And after the ascension of Christ, the Apostles preached the name of Christ, receiving from those who brought. Many villages and acquisitions were sold to the Lord, and their prices were laid before the feet of the Apostles. Ananias was relieved of the price of the village and died with his wife Samphira at the feet of the Apostle Peter. The apostles accepted from those who brought, and tribute from those who demanded, and from there I myself acquired food and clothing. The flesh of their bodies was not made of stone. But you, Strigolnitsa heretics, reproach the eating and drinking of saints and priests, speaking like drones of the Jews of Christ, saying: "They are maneaters and wine-drinkers, friends with publicans and sinners". You heretics say this: "these teachers of music are the ones who eat and drink with the singers, and take from them gold and silver, from the living and the dead. With such evil words you deceive the people. According to your word, the saints and priests are unworthy, but remember the word of the Lord, which he spoke; "on the throne of Moses sit the scribes and Pharisees." Whatever they tell you to do, do it, but do not do it by deed. "For you are to speak, and not create." But you, Strigolnitsy, who revere the Holy Gospel, transgress the word that was spoken: "Repent of the teacher", which Christ himself spoke as a disciple, you consider it a priest's reproach. You do not understand the words of Christ spoken in the Holy Gospel: "Why do you see a speck in your brother's eyes, but do not pick the beams of your own? You hypocrite, you sing louder than the rubbish in your own mind." Remember Paul when he said: "If we had judged ourselves, we would not have been condemned." And again, he said: "Let the lesser of the greater be blessed," like Abraham from Melchizedek. It is not for himself that he receives honor, but for him who is called from God. Not about himself, for this reason, Christ gave the Gospel into the world, so that, by honoring, look at those words, with which to reproach someone, but for this reason, Christ gave the Gospel, so that we may honor ourselves, and reproach ourselves and still govern ourselves. And we see the written word: "All of you understand this, as you are my disciples, if you have love among yourselves." And again, it was said: "Let your light be present, and enlighten before men, and let your deeds be seen for the good they are. Glorify your Father who is in heaven." Having heard this, we do not imagine that before men we are not commanded to boast about virtue: but in the same Gospel that has been found, it is written: "Whenever you fast, do not be like hypocrites, who smear their faces. Whenever you fast, wash your face and anoint your head with oil, so that you do not appear to be a man fasting." Christ commanded everyone to pray in secret in the same way. Vanity and arrogance to run away, not to pray at crossroads and on city streets, nor to exalt bookish words. Christ did not say: "your light is enlightening", but "let your light be enlightening; nothing is secret unless it is revealed. It is not who himself will be glorified, but God himself who will glorify his saints." But you, Strigolnitsy, say that Paul commanded even the common man to teach. By this measure, we all were infidels, and it was not you who were called a heretic, as you are now confusing the faithful Christians, the saints, and the churches of God whom you have offended. Do not be afraid of what is written in Manakon: "Whoever teaches that the Church of God is harmful shall be cursed." You, Strigolnits, ensnare Christians with the word that Christ declared as an Apostle: "Have no brass in your waistbands." Before my passion, I said to them: "When I sent you without a cloak and sandals, did you demand anything?" They came to him: they demanded nothing; Jesus said to them: "Now have shoes and fur." If Christ commanded the disciple to hold the shoes and fur, then is it shameful to hold the shoes and fur? You speak heresies, for behold, you collect many names. It is not you, Strigolnitsy, who judges them. They are judged by God, or by the Great Saint. What are you doing with your head or your foot? Trying to wake up the sheep, becoming a shepherd? And without listening to Gregory the Theologian, who said: "Do not feed the shepherds." You also add this heresy, Strigolnitsy, command all those on earth to repent to its peoples, and not to a priest. Do you not hear the Lord saying: "Confess your sins, pray for each other, that you may be healed?" Therefore the holy Fathers instructed the spiritual fathers, so that the Christians confess to them, just as a sick person declares his harm to the doctor, and the doctor applies a potion to him, according to the evidence of the harm, and heals him.

In the same way the person confesses his sins to the spiritual father, and spiritually the father should command that he cease from that sin, and give him a penance against that sin. Therefore, God will give him that sin. And whoever confesses to the earth, then there is no confession in his confession. The earth is a soulless creature, and we cannot hear and cannot answer, for we cannot stop sinning. Therefore, Christ, our God, will not grant forgiveness of sins to the repentant. This evil net was laid by the devil, Karp the deacon, who did not order them to go to the priest, so that he would take away the priestly honor from the clergy, who had given Christ to bind and absolve sins. The strigolnik themselves were soon bound and excommunicated from the church for his cause of heresy. This leads others to that unconfessed destruction. In the pit of his stomach, he realized that his body would not be buried with psalms and songs. That's why he began to say to people: "it is not worthy to sing over the dead, nor to remember, nor to perform services, nor to bring offerings for the dead to the church, nor to create feasts, nor to give alms for the soul of the deceased." The devil has fallen from his angelic dignity. For this reason, he deceives many people, so that not a single one will be brought to destruction. Thus, the strigolnitsy, who were previously bound, are drawn into their unrighteous bond, so that not one will be bound in heaven and on earth, and excommunicated from the Catholic Church, for the sake of their evil heresies.

It is written that the apostolic rules should be created in memory of the dead. Likewise, the Holy Fathers ordered the remembrance of the departed in every service, and the requiem for them was sung, and the eves of the dead were decreed. Yet, according to heresy, he did not order any offering to be brought, nor a memorial to be commemorated for him. The great church teacher John Chrysostom wrote: "If you did not give alms in your life, give after death, and set your slave free. If you leave your property to your children, write a portion to Christ with your children, so that you can give according to your soul." It is also written in Proloza: "The priest went to the bathhouse to wash, and there was a man serving him. He gave him two proskura, and said: "This bread is holy, it is not for the clergy to eat it, but bring this bread for me to Almighty God. For I am a man who has departed from this light. Even if your prayer for me is heard, you will not find me on the new Sabbath'. Thus, having spoken, he became invisible." Therefore, we understand that these souls themselves ask from us an offering to God. In the books of Pope Gregory it is written: "When you die, have three gold coins. For it was a custom in monasteries to tremble in your cell and then die in drunkenness. When that soul had mercy on the saint, he ordered the ambassador to bring proskura about him every day. On the 30th day, in a dream, I saw him and the elder said: through my prayers, father, my soul was forgiven." And in Kiev, Pechera Anthony, was the only one of them who died in sin and was put in a cave. An evil stench came out of him, and it was revealed to him. The abbot ordered the dog to eat him, after which the prayers of Sts. Anthony and Theodosius and the other saints laid in that tomb, and those living in the monasteries of the holy fathers with prayers from slana. His stench became potent and was transformed into a fragrance. Behold, a sign weakened him. We, the living, therefore, make prayers for the dead. For this reason, God commanded us to pray for each other. Christ, our God, has the power to kill or spare anyone after death. Glory to his great love for mankind and righteous judgment! Hearing the words of Christ: "Beware of the scribes who want to walk in sheep's clothing; inwardly they are wolves and robbers; From their fruit you will know them." And the heretics, the strigolnits, the madmen, say: "they do not plunder the property, they do not collect it." The Pharisees also say: "fasting twice for weeks, without eating all day." The tax collectors, sinners, came to Christ with confession and were saved. Christ said of the Pharisees: "Woe to you scribes, Pharisees and hypocrites! As you pass through sea and land, you ignore the alien. When you encounter one in the geon of fires, they are worse for you." Such is it also with all the heresies, fasting women, prayer mongers and scribes, hypocrites, who are doing clean things only in front of people. If only people had seen their unclean lives, then who would believe their heresies? Or if they had not spoken from the books, who would have listened to them? But in the book scriptures they themselves seduced the heresies, and seduced others from among the unreasonable. About these it has been prophesied: "a stone of stumbling and a stone of offense for those who do not believe in Christ." In the venerable book there is immovable salvation for the faithful. Everyone must revere the book's text, with humility and meekness; and if anyone is reproached with it, and then falls into heresy and is tempted by a stone, the commandment given to him for life is found for him in death. There is something even more marvelous than this: even the demonic ones fast and speak from books, but it is not proper to listen to them. About self-providing teachers, the Apostle said: "For many false prophets have gone out into the world, but do not listen to their words and do not receive them into your homes, lest you commit their evil deeds; the flattering servants are transformed as servants of truth, as Satan himself is transformed into an angel of light." It is also unworthy to listen to Strigolnic teachings. Let no

Christian be caught in the devil's trap, lest he be separated from the immortal source, from the body and blood of the Lord God our Savior Jesus Christ, lest he be condemned to eternal torment. It is worthy for every Christian to come to the Church of God and listen to the singing and readings that are in the holy churches, and to listen to what is written in the Apostle and in the Gospel, which is venerated by the priests. It is unworthy to condemn them, according to what has been said: "Do not condemn, lest you be condemned: if you judge them, you will be condemned." And whoever, according to the Strigolnica heresy, begins to condemn the priest, not only listen to them inappropriately, but also drive them away from the city. The Scripture says: "You will cast out evil from yourselves. It is too little treachery to ferment everything." Christ, our Savior said to his disciples: "Beware of the treachery of the Pharisees," that is, from the teachings of vainglory. For all of these we glorify the Lord God, our Savior, Jesus Christ, who gave us his flesh to eat and his blood to drink, having surrendered to him with the most holy and good and life-giving Spirit, now and ... (*and so on*).

DESK LETTER FROM METROPOLITAN CYPRIAN TO ARCHBISHOP JOHN OF NOVGOROD

On the jurisdiction of the clergy, the inviolability of the Sophia Fatherland and church duties

Cyprian, Metropolitan of Kiev and All Rus', according to the tradition of the saints, the Apostle and the saints, the Father of the Charter, who set the limits of the churches of God, metropolises and bishoprics, and whoever gravitated towards which metropolitans or episcopal monasteries, abbots and monks, priests, and every church person, then everyone is under authority, in obedience to the Saint. Let no one dare, not a single peasant, no matter how small or great, intervene in this matter. If anyone from those abbots, or priests, or monks should be taken away from the Saint by the worldly rulers, such divine rules are cast out and excommunicated. Whoever stands up for them is not blessed. And what about churchyards and villages and lands and waters and duties, what was drawn to the Church of God, or purchases, or who gave their souls to the memory of the deed, but not a single Christian stands up for it. Whoever stands up will not be blessed by the divine rules. For this reason, and the language of Cyprian, Metropolitan of All Rus', according to those divine rules, I gave this letter of mine to the bishop of Novgorod, to St. Sophia, and to my son, the Lord Archbishop of the Great Novgorod Ivan. As long as there are monasteries, let him have abbots in submission and in obedience and the entire priestly rank; also graveyards and villages and land and waters, with all the duties that, under the first Lords, were drawn to that bishopric, to St. Sophia, just as during the first Lords, no matter what was there, so now they are drawn to St. Sophia and to the Lord Ivan. And no one would dare to interfere with church duties, neither in land nor in water, they would fear the execution of the saints; and whoever stood up would have stopped from this hour. And whoever listens to the holy Apostle rules and holy collections of tradition for my teaching, upon that is the mercy of God and His Most Pure Mother and my blessing; and whoever does not listen to my blessing and tries to offend the Church of God, do not receive the mercy of God and His Most Pure Mother, nor my blessing. And the letter was given in Moscow, the month of August on the 29th day.

MESSAGE FROM METROPOLITAN CYPRIAN TO THE PSKOV CLERGY
Transmission by the holy Antimensions, regulations for divine services and synodics, with teachings on how to act during the baptism of infants and the communion of husbands, wives and the sick

Blessing of the Cyprian Metropolitan of Kiev and All Rus', in Pskov, to my children, to the priest assembly of Troyets and Sophia and to all the priests of Pskov. You know that priest Khariton came here to us from you and his comrades to be appointed: and we appointed them and released them; and what you heard, which you do not have the right church rule, then we copied, gave them the charter of the divine services of Chrysostom and Great Basil, also the very service of Chrysostom and the priesthood on the first day of the month of August according to the charter, also the synod, right, true, which revered in Tsarigorod, in St. Sophia, in the patriarchate. Yes, we added to how the Orthodox Tsars should be remembered; also, the Great Princes, both dead and alive, just as we remember here in the metropolis, as well as the baptism of children and every Christian, then betrothal and wedding. And now we haven't had time to write down what you need, otherwise we want to force you to write it easily, and even then, you'll have it; and what was written and sent to you and your brother, that is, everything is right and true. And if I was in Novgorod in Veliky, then I consecrated the antimises, and I ordered the bishop to send those antimises to you too. Now I hear that I myself was with you then, and gave you some of those antimises, and ordered you to cut each antimises in four: otherwise, I did something wrong, to my own destruction. Now Yaz sent with your brother, with the priest with Khariton and his comrades antimisov sixty. In the Troetsk Choir, take over those antimises, and keep them according to the old duty, but consecrate the churches, but do not cut them. Lay them down just as they were cut and decorated and consecrated. And what is natural until now is that children held baptism in their hands, and poured water on top, otherwise it was an incorrect baptism. Now the idea has sent a right baptism, true, according to that nature they themselves would have acted and otherwise they would have ordered everyone to walk according to that. And the Synod I am sent to you by the right Tsaregorodsky, which is why we are here to commemorate, or curse the heretics: and you act accordingly. And to your spiritual children, who are worthy of communion, and want to give communion about the Great Day, or about the Nativity of Christ, or about which Christmastide, as you see worthy; and let's have lunch. As the deacon says: "approach with the fear of God and in faith," then they would come to the royal doors and receive communion in front of the royal doors, with their hands placed crosswise to their feathers, but they would not touch the sovereign; Also, give communion to the wives without finishing the mass, but would take communion at other doors that are opposite the altar, unless only to a sick person: otherwise, to the sick person, and go into the courtyard, give communion; and men would not come to Holy Communion wearing votols, but would take off their votols; and on whom a guard or a fur coat would be useful, and would be belted. And God's mercy is upon you. And the letter was given in Moscow, in the month of April on the 17th day.

Letter from Metropolitan Cyprian to the Pskovites
About the non-judgment of priests without a saintly court and the non-appropriation of villages and church lands

These are the words of Cyprian, Metropolitan of Kiev and All Rus'. What have I heard, even in Pskov the laity judge priests and execute them in church things, otherwise, that is, except for the Christian law: it is not fit for a lay priest to judge or execute, or condemn him, not to say a word to him: but who puts them up, the Saint, but them and judge and execute and teach. And you, my children, Pskovites, from great to small, would naturally not judge the priests, nor execute them, would naturally not have a sin on their souls, nor would they make a pledge for the whole of Pskov. I also heard that some young priests were widowed, and neither left the priesthood nor got married; and it is also unsuitable for you to judge them, so that they are not naturally deprived of anything. The Saint knows that whoever appoints them, he is the one who appoints them and casts them out and judges and executes and teaches; and it's not good for you to intervene in that matter. And whoever the Church of God and the Saint announces, and according to that announcement it is appropriate for you to hold him in the same way. And what about the church lands and villages, whether they bought them, or who gave them, dying, to which churches; and in your nature, no one from you would intercede, so that the Church of God would not be harmed, for this is a great sin from God. For this reason, according to the rank and region that God has given me, I teach you my children, and you listen to my word; and whoever does not listen to this letter, does not receive God's mercy on him or my blessing; or whoever listens, and God's mercy is on you. And the charter was given in Veliky Novgorod, the month of May on the 12th day, index 5, in the year 6903.

LETTER FROM METROPOLITAN CYPRIAN TO THE PSKOVITES

The destruction of the charter given to them by the Bishop Dionysius of Suzdal, and the observance of the charter of Grand Duke Alexander in the old days

These are the words of Cyprian, Metropolitan of Kiev and All Rus'. What have I heard, already Vladyka of Suzhdal Denisey copied the letter when he was in Pskov, and added to the letter the Great Prince Alexandrov, on what to go, how to judge, or how to execute whom, and wrote down and a curse, who has the wrong walk; Otherwise, Vladyka Denis did not do his own thing, not according to the law and not according to the rule. Once the charter has been created, the Great Prince Alexander decided what to follow: and every Tsar in his kingdom, or a Prince in his reign, is free to manage every matter and write down the charters. Also, that Great Prince Alexander in his reign, and copied such a letter, according to which he is free to follow the Christian good. And that

Vladyka Denisiy got involved in something other than his own business, and copied an inappropriate letter, and I am destroying that evil letter. And you, my children, Pskovites, even before this you walked according to that charter of the Great Prince Alexander, and then you have the old days: and you walk according to that old times; and what about the missive Denisyev's letter, send that letter to me, and I'll take that myself: that letter is not a letter. And that I wrote a curse and unblessing to the patriarch, otherwise I remove the curse from you and bless you: that was the Lord of Suzdal, and he acted in a time of rebellion; but the Patriarch did not order him to do this. But you, my children, walk according to your duty, and judge the courts according to the old times; and whoever is guilty, worry about it, of course; show what guilt is against him, worry about it, of course; act in the old way, purely and without sin, like all Christians. And God's mercy is upon you and my blessing. And the charter was given in Veliky Novgorod, May 12, Indiction 5, in the summer of 6903.

METROPOLITAN CYPRIAN'S TEACHING TO THE CLERGY
About church services, about non-admission to the holy secrets of thieves and murderers without repentance, about penances, nepotism, non-communication with those who ridicule, about the purity of men and cases of those who interrupt during the service

Cyprian, by the grace of God, Metropolitan of Kiev and all Russia. Naturally they asked me about the services of Great Basil, be it known to you: the service of Great Basil begins in the second week of Lent; and on the week of the raw food service, Chrysostom's service, as well as on the week of collection, before the synodical is read for the collection, the Chrysostom service is also held; and from the second week of Lent, into Great Lent, for every week, serve the Great Basil's service. Chrysostom's service at the lyre's maiden; and for the canon of the Nativity of Christ, and for the canon of St. Basil's baptism of the Great service. Many people honor the work of the Great Basil and serve on his feast day. And on Wednesday of Shrovetide week and on Friday there are no services, but only hours with vespers; also on Good Friday for this reason. And then, at the time of death, the murderer gives communion, but even when they repent, they tell all their sins purely. But how can one give communion to a non-repentant? But the church does not have any second priesthood, except if the holy throne is damaged, then sacredness is needed, then all sorts of things are needed anew. And on Great Saturday evening, there is no Methymon at all. And what naturally they asked me: even if the deacon is not useful, is it necessary for many priests to sing together, so that from which priest the young one can become a deacon? There is neither youth nor oldness in the populace, but it is not worth it to be; and if it were to make a priest a deacon, otherwise there would be neither a priest nor a deacon, then it cannot be so: a priest is a priest, and a deacon is a deacon; and if there is no need for a deacon, the priest will serve alone. Why are you asking if "Holy God" is sung at the altars: sometimes there are congregations of churches, but the priests are Kriloshans with deacons without change [...] on the way out, to the altars: and the singers sing "Holy God," and "Glory," they sing "even now," and the priests sing in the altars only the last one, "Holy God." And at the Elevation of the Honest Cross in every church, throughout the whole earth where Christians live, the Cross is raised, even if only one priest was, for the glory of the Honest and Life-Giving Cross. And whose spiritual father cannot bless a person for his disobedience, and he lives for a year, and is not known, does not repent, and comes to death and never repents, it is not worthy to give him holy communion; and he begins to roll before death and cry, confessing his guilt, otherwise accept him in repentance and give him communion, and even death will be useful to him, then it will be a matter of what he will be put in; but only to recover from this illness and be healthy, otherwise he will get drunk for his previous business. About nepotism, that a child should be baptized by his godfather and his godfather, there is no such thing: it is inappropriate to baptize two, neither a husband with another man's wife, nor with his own wife, but it is suitable for one to baptize, either from the male sex, or from the female. And why are you asking us about the rostrigi, and I am amazed at this: every Christian knows that even if he is a Christian, if he denies Christ, then it is not good for him to eat or drink, or kiss him, or meet with him, so run away from him; Likewise, whoever mocks the angelic image and overthrows himself, he is like him, and the divine rules command so, with such people neither eat nor drink, nor hold any customs; and whoever does not repent, does not take on the angelic image again, the divine rules curse him. And even if someone is appointed to the priesthood and deaconship, he must be as pure as he was born from his mother's womb, there would be no better vow to make. And then some kind of attack happens in the priesthood or in the diaconate, due to the devil's inspiration, otherwise he will cease from service at that hour; There is no drink for him, but just don't drink until he dies. This is a lesson to you from me. And

God's mercy is upon you. And a list was given in Novgorad, in the summer of 6903.

MESSAGE FROM THE BELOZERSK MONASTERY OF ABBOT KIRILL TO THE GRAND DUKE VASILY DIMITRIEVICH
Asking him to reconcile with the Suzdal Princes

To the faithful and God-loving Prince Great Vasily Dmiteyevich, Kirilo, who has sinned so much with his brother, on yours, sir, who is pleased with your mercy for us, we beat our heads a lot, and we rejoice, sir, in you, that you have great faith in the Most Pure Mother of God and our poverty and about your great humility. For this, sir, we rejoice and grieve, more than words and meaning, your immeasurable humility: you send to me, a sinner and a beggar, and every good deed who has withdrawn. You, sir, are the Great Prince of the entire Russian land, and in humility, you send to me, sinful and passionate and unworthy, heaven and earth and that same monastic life; and I, sir, a sinner, truly grieve for this, unworthiness for the sake of my own, but we rejoice, sir, for the goodness of your will and humbly-wise disposition, as you have become like this, sir, our most good Master and Lord, from the amount of ineffable glory and from above who came down for us for the sake of sinners and humbled himself even to the point of being a servant of the image. Sitsa, sir, and you, from the great glory of this world, bow with humility to our poverty, and from this, sir, we recognize your great love for God and His Most Pure Mother. As much as the Saints approach God with love, only as they see themselves as sinners; For, sir, with this humility you greatly gain salvation and spiritual progress. Therefore, sir, I am a sinner with a sadder soul, because you please me, unworthy and resigned to every sin, not possessing a single virtue, but guilty of every passion, and thus, sir, you send a prayer to me, who is unable to pray to God for my sins. And how about you, sir, will I pray to God, since I myself am filled with every deed of evil? But, sir, it is written that he does not order sinners to deny themselves and to pray to God for those who command for them, for the sake of their faith. At the same time, sir, for the sake of your great faith, God will not leave you, but will have mercy on you, and the Most Pure Lady Theotokos and our Queen will help you all the days of your life and will give you healing of soul and body, that you do not forget us her beggars, sir. in this empty place, gathered in her monastery, but you often look at them with contented alms. We, sir, cannot repay you anything for this, but the Most Pure Lady Theotokos, our hope and hope, will ask for mercy from her Son for you in this age and in the future. And the sinful language with your brother, sir, there is great strength. I am glad to pray to God for you, our lord, and for your Princess and for your children and for all the peasants entrusted to you by God. But you, sir, for God's sake, take heed to yourself and to all your reign, and place the Holy Spirit in it to shepherd the people of the Lord, acquisition of honest blood. As you have been vouchsafed by God, you owe much greater reward. So repay your debt to the Benefactor, keeping His holy commandments, turning away from everyone who leads to destruction. As with ships, when a mercenary, even an oarsman, is seduced, he does little harm to those sailing with him; but with the helmsman, then he does the whole ship is set to destruction: the same, sir, about the Princes. If someone sins against the boyars, he does not do harm to all people, but only to himself alone; Or else the Prince himself does harm to all people like him. But you, sir, guard yourself with great firmness in good deeds; the holy Apostle said: "Have peace and holiness, without it no one will see the Lord." Hate, sir, all of the powers that draw you to sin. Have an immutable pious thought and do not rise, sir, with temporary glory to vain vacillation: for the life that exists here is small and short, and death is associated with the flesh. And if you think about this, do not fall into the pit of pride: but fear, sir, God, the true King, and you will be blessed: "Blessed are those who fear the Lord." Remember, sir, the hope of the future age and the kingdom of heaven, the joy of the Saints, the joy of the Angels, everyone must see the sweet face of God; for there is truly unspeakable kindness, all the sweetness and desire and insatiable love for all who love him and do his most holy will. "Yes, you have heard, Mr. Great Prince, that there is great confusion between you and your relatives, the Princes of Suzdal." You, sir, tell your truth, and they tell theirs; and in that, sir, between you peasants there is great bloodshed. Otherwise, sir, look truly at what their truth will be before you, and you, sir, act on yourself with your humility; and what will be your truth before them, and you, sir, stand for yourself in truth. And if you, sir, began to beat you with your forehead, and you, sir, for God's sake, would have granted them according to their measure; before, sir, I heard that you had needs before, and that is why, sir, they forbade you. And you, sir, for God's sake, show them your love and salary, so that they do not perish in error in the Tatar countries, and they do not die there. Without it, sir, neither the kingdom, nor the reign, nor any other power can deliver us from the impersonal judgment of

God; And if, sir, to love your neighbor as yourself, and to comfort the sorrowing and embittered soul, sir, it will help a lot at the terrible and righteous judgment of Christ, as Apostle Paul, a disciple of Christ, writes: "If the imam removes the faith from the mountains, and if the imam gives away all his property "I am not a teacher of love, I am nothing." The Beloved writes to John the Theologian: "If anyone says, I love God, but I hate my brother, it is a lie." In the same way, sir, love the Lord God with all your soul; Thus love your brothers and all the peasants: and thus, sir, your faith in God and your alms to the poor will be pleasing to God. And may the mercy of God and the Most Pure Mother of God be on you, on my master on Grand Duke Vasily, and on your Grand Duchess, and on your children, and my blessing and prayer and my brothers. Amen.

The Scriptorium Project is the work of a small group of lay people of various apostolic churches who are interested in the preservation, transmission, and translation of the works of the early and medieval church. Our efforts are to make the works of the church fathers accessible to anyone who might have an interest in Christian antiquities and the theological, philosophical, and moral writings that have become the bedrock of Western Civilization.

To-date, our releases have pulled from the Greek, Syriac, Georgian, Latin, Celtic, Ethiopian, and Coptic traditions of Christianity, and have been pulled from sundry local traditions and languages.

www.ingramcontent.com/pod-product-compliance
Lightning Source LLC
LaVergne TN
LVHW061605070526
838199LV00077B/7185